Scent of Jasmine

Scent of Jasmine

Nitza Agam

Dedication page

To my supportive and loving husband, Ofer,

    my sons who I appreciate and love every day, David and Orr.

To my mother, Naomi,
who encouraged me to write and to love books,
and to all my women friends who embrace me in a loving circle.

Acknowledgements

A special thank you to friends Dr. Abigail Caplin and Jen Vaida for their invaluable help with the editing process.

Thank you to Catherine Herrera for the cover photo.

Cover photo by Catherine Herrera/Flor de Miel Fotos, 2011. www.catherineherreraphotography.com

Biography

Writing has always been Nitza's form of expression, ever since she received her first diary which was a Girl Scout journal with a thick, silver lock at the age of eight. Nitza was born in New Jersey and left at the age of eighteen to immigrate to Israel and attend Hebrew University in Jerusalem. It was in Israel during the 1973 Yom Kippur War that her life transformed. Her fiancé was killed during the first week in the Sinai Desert at the age of twenty four. Nitza was twenty two at the time, and realized then that she had to write about the war and document it in some way. It would become a way of healing from the terrible grief and loss. After living in Israel and receiving her degree, as well as performing in children's theatre and a woman's theatre group, she left Israel for San Francisco and has remained there since. She holds two master degrees in literature from San Francisco State and has been a teacher of English since 1981 in various independent schools in the Bay Area. She married her husband, Ofer, in 1980, and had two sons, David and Orr, in 1983 and 1985. Her husband was diagnosed with MS in 1980; since then they have lived with the many challenges of that illness, as well as learned how to appreciate the many joys of life.

Scent of Jasmine was written as a memoir to capture the pivotal moments in prose and poetry of the three settings where Nitza has lived: New Jersey, Israel, and San Francisco. As a fellow colleague wrote about Nitza and why she writes: "Nitza uses memoir to educate, to illuminate, and to simply share-her words enrich her community as well. Nitza is able to take her life experiences-losing a fiancé to war, the experience of war, the joys of friendship, the awakening of her sexuality, bidding farewell to aging parents and burying them, supporting a husband through the debilitation of MS, the challenges of parenting and of giving birth-to give us all a sense of purpose, and a sense of common humanity." (Jen Vaida: colleague at St. Joseph's of the Sacred Heart.)

Simply put, it has been Nitza's way to share her life and to affirm all those moments that define us, large and small. No experience is minor; whether it is a ride on a motorcycle, trick or treating through a New Jersey neighborhood, the way her mother made tuna fish sandwiches, or losing her fiancé to war.

Nitza has published poems and essays in magazines such as *Poetica, Reed* (San Jose State literary magazine,) *Bridges: a Jewish Feminist Journal,* (2009) and in *The San Francisco Chronicle,* and various educational journals.

Table of Contents

Scent of Jasmine: 1973

The tanks rolled down the highway perched on trucks, or drove on their own. I had never seen a tank before, and now there were so many. Our bus went one way. They went in the opposite direction heading south to the desert. Traffic was slow. We inched along as we passed a long convoy of heavy machinery. The tanks seemed like headless horsemen without their champion warriors. I thought about how Michael hated tanks, and wondered if he was in one of them.

Tel Aviv was like a ghost town. I walked the empty streets, thinking, wondering, and imagining those tanks moving endlessly on the highway. Tanks were supposed to make their way in sand, not on concrete highways. Yet, they had to be transported there somehow. When I was five years old, I had my tonsils out. I dreamt of a pack of cards showing themselves to me, card after card: jacks, queens, and kings, each card appeared larger and larger and then disappeared. This is my only memory of the ether-produced dreams. I recall hearing voices telling me to breathe deeply, one breath after another. I would breathe and see a card as it appeared before me before making way for the next card. Just like the tanks.

My grandparent's house was a refuge. I wanted to sit in their living room, drink my grandmother's sweet coffee, and eat her apple strudel. I wanted to wake up from an afternoon nap to find her knitting and to feel her soft skin against my cheek. I wanted to believe everything would be all right. But I couldn't eat, I couldn't drink, and I couldn't sleep. All I could do was walk the deserted streets and imagine those tanks, empty and headless.

I couldn't stay in Tel Aviv. I hitched a ride to the desert town where Michael and I lived. It didn't take me long to get there.

His motorcycle was parked outside the door of our two-room cabin. He had left it there the day the war broke out. I remembered how disappointed we had been about not being able to make love for a few days because a friend of mine was visiting with us, and we hadn't wanted to make noise. We finally broke down that night before he left. I was glad. I found a postcard from him mailed a few days before from somewhere in the south. It was brief. "I'm fine. Miss you. Take this to my mother and let her know I'm O.K."

A soldier picked me up on my way to his mother's house. Hitching was easy. It was the best way to get around during a war. Everyone picked anyone up whether they were soldiers or not. The soldier who offered me a ride was Yemenite: dark, with a mustache, and not that young, probably in his late twenties or early thirties. He told me that he was a photographer and needed to stop by his house, which was on the way. He asked if it was all right with me. I was fine with it. I just wanted to get there.

The photographer's name was Gideon. His house was situated in the middle of a garden courtyard full of fruit trees and thick with the scent of jasmine. I wished I could hide in this idyllic garden with this dark, sexy soldier who began to fall in love with me. He described how many weddings he had photographed in that very garden. Did I want him to photograph Michael and me? He would be happy to, he said. As soon as Michael got home, he would arrange it. "Did I want to marry?" he asked. It seemed he wanted to both seduce me and marry me off. Suddenly, I was not so sure I wanted to rush to Michael's mother's house.

He leaned towards me. He told me how beautiful I was, and asked whether I really needed to get anywhere so soon. His voice seemed safe and warm, his hands felt good, and the scent of jasmine, lemon, and orange trees made me think of lying down and feeling him on top of me.

"You will have your wedding in my garden, and I will photograph the two of you," he whispered in my ear, "soon, very soon." I wanted to believe him, to make love to him, and to know that Michael was coming back, and that maybe we would get married in this garden.

I looked around his home. I was astonished to find photographs of famous Israeli celebrities and politicians: Golda Meir, Yitzhak Rabin, and Shimon Peres. I was surrounded by faces one only saw on television or read about in the newspaper—this photographer was obviously renown. I found the presence of the faces crowded in his living room overwhelming. Books were strewn everywhere. His shelves were packed with books. More books lay on the floor, on his desk, and next to his bed. A thick, bright sofa was in the middle of his living room, not far from his desk. His bedroom was messy—cluttered with newspapers on the floor, coffee cups next to his bed, and an unmade bed. Or perhaps it was wartime, and he didn't have time to straighten up. Was this who he was or a reflection of the war?

We sat on the sofa, and his arm rested on my knee. He caressed my arm as we spoke. His touch felt light, sensual, and slow. I thought; why not sink into this sofa with these light caressing hands and warm voice, surrounded by photos of famous people and personal items of a stranger's life, and the strong, ever-present scent of jasmine.

"Somehow," he said, "I feel close to you and to Michael. I can picture you in my house, my garden. There is something special about you, about the both of you. I promise you, you will get married here, and I will photograph you." As he spoke, his hand ran up and down my arm.

I tried to imagine it. I loved Michael, but I was afraid of making the commitment to marriage. I wondered if I was too young, or if I might never be able to commit to one man. I just knew that I wanted Michael back, and then I could think about marriage. On the other hand, this photographer felt so comforting, so sexy, so promising, so safe; and the here and now was all that mattered. This garden, this living room, this hand, his mouth, this moment—could make me forget my anxiety and my sleepless nights.

He began to kiss me and lick my ear, and slowly unbuttoned my blouse. We began to kiss and I felt his tongue in my mouth exploring slowly, ever so slowly. How had I gotten here? I wanted to tell him I had to go. I had to bring Michael's postcard to his mother. She needed to know he was safe. My blouse was off as he played with my breasts and continued to kiss me.

"You're very beautiful, very special. Are you sure you're not Yemenite? With your dark eyes, dark hair, and dark skin. You could be," he said.

I thought of Michael's room, and the bed we had made love in just a few nights before. How we always wanted each other, always had to touch each other whenever we met, and how we usually always went to bed before anything else. I loved his blue eyes, his soft beard, the slight protrusion of his stomach, and I could never tire of looking at him, watching him when he slept, waking up to reach out and touch him, and to make love again, over and over again. What had he taken with him when he left? A rifle and an apple and a toothbrush in his small army duffel bag. We kissed quickly and then he was gone. I began to tape the windows with black cloth for possible black-outs or bombing attacks, as the neighbors had instructed. One minute we had laughed about something, and within half an hour, he was in his army uniform, walking out the door.

Now, this stranger was kissing me just a few days later. I wanted to give in to his soft lingering kisses, and let my desire take over. But how could I? How did I get here? I was standing on the road determined to get to Michael's mother's house and show her the postcard as soon as possible, but I had taken a detour with this unknown Yemenite photographer who lived alone in a charming home in the middle of a garden courtyard near the ocean.

The image of the tanks, one after another, paraded before me. Michael's motorcycle parked in front of our home, and the old dreamlike pictures of the playing cards appeared before me. I kept seeing our room, our bed, and the pictures of us plastered all over the small room. Michael had a few photographs he had taken of me taped above his desk. I looked exotic and melancholy but happy. I couldn't always recognize myself. Who was this young woman so in love, and now in the arms of someone else in the middle of a war?

A few days ago, everything seemed so normal, so right. Other than not being able to make love when we wanted because of my friend's visit, we had no problems. I had pushed the question of marriage away and felt I had time to work out my fears and doubts. Now time was something else. I wasn't able to sleep or eat, or remember one minute to the next. Just knowing how to get from one place to another: from Tel Aviv to Beer -Sheva, from Beer - Sheva to Rehovot, was confusing.

I had not had other lovers, though I had thought of it a few times. It worried me that even though I was so in love with Michael, I thought about other men and had been tempted to kiss them and experiment. I was ashamed of my feelings; I could not share them with Michael. He had asked me a few times about my attraction to other men, when I was studying in Jerusalem and spent the week away from him. I vehemently denied any such attractions. Now, in the arms of Gideon, pictures of wildflowers that Michael loved to photograph came to me; red, white, pink, blooming in the desert, even in the snowfall that had taken our desert city by surprise. They bloomed. They flourished. He loved taking pictures of flowers. Michael had loved nature and flowers while Gideon was intrigued by celebrities. It felt surreal that during a war, I would find myself surrounded by photographs in this strange cottage kissed by one while thinking of the other.

I knew I had to get away and leave this house before something happened that I would regret. "Please, let's just go, and take me to Michael's mother's home. I should have been there hours ago. We need to go." While he was reluctant to leave, he heard the urgency in my voice, and understood that nothing more sexual would happen between us.

We got back into his car and left. It was difficult for me to look at him and hear his voice, as he tried to reassure me and soothe me about my fears for Michael's safety.

The roads were empty: no tanks, no warriors, merely empty highways that spoke of a country in limbo, just like I was. I was not in Tel Aviv with my grandparents, not in Beer-Sheva, which was our home, and not in Rehovot, which was Michael's mother's home. I was on the road with a stranger who looked at me with lust in his eyes and spoke in a velvet voice. Where was I? Who was I? A few days ago I was on the back of a motorcycle looking out at the desert feeling the wind in my face, and life had seemed fairly simple.

The industrial city of Rehovot welcomed us as we entered the main streets. Michael's mother lived in a residential neighborhood near the famous scientific institute, which was enclosed, wooded, green, and lush. He wanted to take me right to the house. I asked him to drop me off nearby. I wanted to walk there by myself, and I wanted us to part. "Please let me know how everything is," he said. "Can I take your number, and call you to make sure you're alright?"

"Sure," I answered--anything to just go and put this behind me. I wrote down my grandparent's number and gave it to him. "Thanks," I murmured, slamming the door behind me. I did not look back.

I walked the few blocks to Michael's mother's house. It was familiar, as he and I had often walked these streets before. I had come here first, to meet him, before he had moved to Beer-Sheva. This was his childhood home, and the home of his first girlfriend. Sometimes I was jealous of her, since they were still friends. I had seen her once or twice, and she was beautiful. An airline stewardess who worked for El-Al, and she seemed more confident than me. She was part Russian and part Yemenite, and sultry and sexy. Jealousy would overtake me, and I needed to have Michael reassure me that I was his only love. Even if I secretly yearned after others, I wanted to know that he desired only me.

It was early evening, and the streets were still. Usually I loved to take a walk or sit in a café this time of day. Now, the streets were empty. People sat in their homes watching television with their families, wondering about their brothers, sons, husbands, and lovers. I took the postcard out of my bag. The handwriting was so familiar, and while it had seemed rushed, the simple sentences soothed me, "I'm fine. I love you. Bring this to my mother."

I had called before to tell them I was on my way, so they would expect me. I knocked on the door. I don't know who opened it. The living room was full of people. I noticed that Michael's mother was kneeling on the floor, her head bent as if in prayer. This confused me. I knew his mother was not religious: what was she doing on the floor in that position? All eyes turned towards me; there was silence.

Then, one of Michael's next door neighbors, who we had spoken to occasionally, a harried blonde mother with two children, looked at me. I stared at her, at her eyes. I noticed the door of his room was closed. I knew that room intimately. It was his childhood room, and contained a single bed, a desk, some of his childhood souvenirs, and photos. We had made love in that bed, and once his mother had walked in on us. I was so embarrassed and humiliated that she had "caught" us. He merely laughed, and said that it did not affect her. They had a mature relationship, but they were not close. He had lost his father at an early age, and as a single mother with three children to raise; she had tried her best, but was never loving and warm or maternal. They were more like "friends" than mother and son.

I looked back at the neighbor. Then she said it. It seemed scripted, as my response to her seemed scripted. "Michael was killed today. He is dead."

I felt as if I were in a movie. My response seemed so pat, so on cue. "No, no, no, it can't be." It can't be, No, no, no, no."

I just kept repeating no over and over again and looking at this closed door. It was the sight of his door that made me realize that he was dead, not what the neighbor had said and the sight of so many people, just the closed door, which I knew, would not open. He wasn't going to walk through that door, and we were not going to make love anymore.

I stood there in the open doorway of his apartment staring at the door to his room. I was crying, but not deeply. It was as if I was in a movie and my tears and words were scripted. Were these words coming out of my mouth? Where had I heard them? They seemed so trite, so unreal. And yet, there they were. I don't remember being held, embraced, caressed, or comforted. I called Annemarie, my South African friend who lived in Tel Aviv with her husband and young child. She and I were close friends, and the four of us had recently taken a trip together to the Sinai Desert. Michael and I had often sat in their living room drinking coffee or tea or beer, listening to music and talking politics. I needed to hear her voice, but she was pregnant with her second child and I worried that the shock might affect her. I called her and made sure she was sitting down before I told her the news. She told me she'd be right over.

I didn't want to go to my grandparents which was where I would stay. They lived a half hour from Michael's mother's home, and I knew this would devastate them. They loved him so, and looked forward to our wedding. I couldn't face them, yet. My parents were abroad, and I knew that Annemarie would help me get through this night. The next thing I remember is sleeping with Annemarie on a mattress on her floor. She held me the entire night. She held me close, and let me cry. She comforted me, and I don't remember talking, just the sense of her warm loving presence next to me. Her large stomach touched me, and the signs of life inside of her contrasted my reality.

Somehow, after being held by her that night, I was able to get through the next day and inform my parents, who were visiting in the U.S., my friends, and my grandparents. There was no funeral or memorial service. A war was being waged, and soldiers were killed and wounded. Those who were killed were buried in a temporary military cemetery. Families would be informed about the location of the cemetery after the war. Only then could they find the marker, the number, and the name that signified the person. Funeral services were a luxury that war did not afford until the war was over.

I stayed at my grandparent's home in Tel-Aviv. My women friends descended on me, and surrounded me with their love. I was grateful for their touch and their caresses. It was so important for me to touch and be touched. It made that horrible emptiness more bearable.

That next day, Gideon called to see how I was. He had no idea that Michael had been killed. He was simply calling to check on me and see if I had delivered the postcard which was still in my bag, of course. I didn't know what to do with it. I couldn't give it to her. I never gave it to her. I told him simply what had happened. He wanted to immediately come to see me. I couldn't see him. I wanted to escape into his garden as I had done before, but now there was no fantasy of wedding plans to make. I wanted Michael back. I wanted us to make love again. How could I want him when he was dead? I might think of the scent of jasmine and the ocean which was not far away, and the photographer's courtyard which enclosed the small home and had for a brief moment, seemed to protect me. I had rested there, not knowing I was on my way to find out that Michael had been killed near his tank. His lungs had been blown away, shattered like the glass of a car window, with so many tiny splinters.

A few days before the war broke out, the front window of our Volvo had been inexplicably shattered. We had parked it in front of my house, and a few hours later, we found it broken. It had horrified me. Now, I thought, the shattered glass was like Michael's lungs, torn into minute pieces. I was glad that he had not been inside his tank. He hated tanks. He loved flowers and nature.

I dreamed about Michael for many years after the war. In my dreams, I would try to call him on the phone and he would not answer. I would see his face under a helmet on a motorcycle on the Israeli highways. I would see myself holding onto him, tightly. I would feel the wind in our faces, smell the desert wind, the sage and the brush. Sometimes, looking out a bus window, I would cry, thinking of him, remembering him. I never cried in bed or in my room, but always on buses. The only other times I cried was when I made love with men I didn't know very well. I cried often. It would take me many years to fall in love again, and even then, I would cry, when making love.

Prayer in a Bunker

Baruch Ata Adonai Elohenu
Blessed be thou God O Lord
keep us safe
keep me safe
keep my friends safe
keep my lover safe
I don't know what else to say

A suburban Israeli neighborhood
with nice newer cars, apartments, supermarkets
well paved streets, lemon trees—
sounds of children playing, their happy shouts
as they are picked up from daycare
in pink-orange
twilight hours;
their Hebrew voices lilt to their names—
Avigail, Tal, Ophir,
Sarit, Daniel, David, Shachar, Tal, Ora.

My friends and I sit in a bunker
We are foreigners.
from South Africa
and New Jersey.
We never planned to sit in bunkers
or learn how to pray.

Two weeks ago,
we shopped in the Bedouin market
for fresh fruits and vegetables,
watched the sunset in the desert
felt the wind on our faces,
Annemarie's very pregnant belly protruded.

Another plea comes to mind:
Please let Michael live.
Don't let him be killed.
Let him be wounded—
the injury doesn't have to be bad,
he needn't lose a limb
or be paralyzed.

Baruch Ata Adonai Elohenu Melech HaOlam,
Blessed be God, Lord of the Universe,
a blessing you say over bread or wine
not a plea bargain in a bunker in the middle of a war.

Shema Yisrael Adonai Elohenu Adonai Ehad.
Hear O Israel, God is one.
This cornerstone of devotion, obedience, faith.

Jews chanted as they marched to gas chambers.
I can't say it.

When we emerge from the bunker
I am so relieved.

In two days,
I will enter my fiancé's apartment
see his mother knelt in prayer on the living room floor.

I will walk in and stare
at the closed door of his room.

In thirty days, we recite the Kaddish.
It is hard to get the words out.

Van Gogh Museum, Amsterdam, Holland: 1974

It seemed to always rain in Holland. My memories of Holland as a child when my family lived in Rotterdam for two months during the summer were of rain and gray clouds. It was a picture perfect kind of country: orderly, calm, and filled with friendly people. Tulips were growing everywhere. There were lots of canals, and lots and lots of bicycles. I loved the red geraniums on the windows, the delicious cheese and chocolate, the tall Victorian style houses close to one another. It was quaint and historic and picturesque. This time, all I could do in Holland was cry. I walked up and down the stairs in the Van Gogh Museum. His famous paintings of flowers and landscapes and people were imprinted in my mind, and I felt grateful to be in such a special spot; I looked out at the rainy landscape of the city through the tall glass windows and cried. I was twenty three years old, and this was my first trip out of Israel after the 1973 War when Michael was killed. I thought it would be good for me to travel and get out of the country where he inhabited every corner, and everywhere I looked I was struck with our images and memories.

Perhaps I could forget, once I left the familiar Israeli landscape, where we had made love in every part of the country. The last time I had left the country, it was against Michael's wishes and with his disapproval. He could not understand my need to travel without him, to spend time with a good girlfriend, and be away from him for a month. Why was I abandoning him? Why couldn't I wait for him so we could travel together? Isn't that what people in love did: spend most of their time together and certainly not seek imposed separations? But, I wanted not to be "in love" for a bit, and not feel the intensity of our relationship, not worry about "us," not think how to behave or what to say, but to just laugh and be free with my friend. I liked arriving at the American Express offices all over Europe to receive his love letters. I liked missing him and him missing me. I could acknowledge our love but still have my freedom, my need to be with women friends, and with myself. Separation would only enhance our relationship, make it better and stronger.

That was in 1972, a year before the war broke out. A year later would be the summer before the war: our last time together as a couple, as unknowingly, the country moved toward a war that would kill many, injure thousands, and take Michael's life in a bomb attack out on the desert as he tried to save comrades who were dodging bombs. He would not be so lucky; the explosion of one bomb would hemorrhage his lungs, and hopefully, he did not know that he was fatally injured when he passed out and later died.

Now I had my freedom, and no love of my life. I was free, as I had wanted to be during the summer of 1972. Amsterdam was the first stop on this healing trip. I felt more abandoned than ever before. I had not chosen my freedom. I struggled with my bizarre relief at having the freedom and the terrible guilt that it was given to me in this fashion. I had always been afraid of the commitment of the relationship, of marriage, of vows that bound me to another person forever. Was I being punished for wanting my freedom?

No one knew why I was crying. I am not sure they cared. They saw a young tourist, dark and thin, backpack on her back, looking out the rain soaked windows and crying. Van Gogh could not comfort me. The tulips and bicycles and friendly Dutch people could not comfort me. I wanted Michael back. I wanted to be in love again and make love and ride on the back of his motorcycle and feel the wind in my face and smell the eucalyptus that pervaded Israel.

Amsterdam was not the city of my youth. I felt the rain and the loneliness and the seediness of it. The red light district of the city had prostitutes posed in windows; women of all shapes and sizes dressed in sexy lingerie on sale for the right price. What choices did they have about love and freedom? Some of those women were my age. My purse had been stolen. The museum was cold and lifeless despite the colors of the paintings. I was alone. I missed Michael, and I felt sorry for myself. I had it all and it was taken away from me. What would I do with this freedom now that I had it? How would I live the rest of my life?

Public Places, Private Spaces: 1973

I heard the sound before I got there. I didn't know what it was. Soon I realized it was the sound of thousands of people crying. The sound increased as we approached in our car. The 1973 War had been over for a week. It was a month since the war began, which had lasted for three weeks. The families of those killed in the war had been notified and given some opportunity to mourn: this was their chance to claim their loved one, in a large lot not far from Tel-Aviv.

The graves were marked with numbers. No names. You had to find the number of your loved one much like in a lottery or a seat in an auditorium. Eventually, each family would move these family members: sons, lovers, friends, husbands, brothers, uncles, to a permanent grave and cemetery of the families' choosing. I knew that Michael's body would be moved to lie next to his father in the city where he was born. I had visited that grave with him not too long ago and had been shocked to see how young his father had been when he was killed in a motorcycle accident. Now, Michael would be buried next to him, not much younger than his father was.

Michael had quickly left our cottage when the war broke out in the desert city, Beer-Sheva, taking an apple, a toothbrush, and his rifle. He dressed in his uniform, gave me a quick kiss good-bye, and I was left to put black cloth over the windows on my own. I was left to consider my first war experience and to worry about his safety. I never thought he would die.

I worried that he might be wounded or lose a leg or an arm. Since he loved to ride his motorcycle all over the country, that would impede his passion for freedom and his desire to have the wind on his face. I tried to plan how I would act or feel in the face of mutilation or any kind of injury. I did not plan for his death.

After the war was over, his comrades who had served with him in the tank paid me a bereavement visit. They described his fatal injury: the sound of an explosion nearby which had hemorrhaged his lungs. He had fainted and had to be taken away. He died soon after. He had still looked perfect: that sculpted face, bright blue eyes that were now closed, a dirty blonde beard and full head of hair. His face was peaceful, like he was asleep. There was no sign of war: no blood, or any kind of wound. It was as if he was just permanently asleep.

We thought we would get married in the spring; instead I was looking for his number on a temporary marker in a makeshift cemetery surrounded by the sound of thousands of people crying and screaming: the sound of a nation's grief.

My brother led us to the spot. He seemed so much calmer than the rest of us; I could not have made it without him. I could not have withstood the sound of all the screaming and sobbing that engulfed us in one long wail of human misery and grief. Families stood over these markers, and because some of the families were from Arab speaking countries, the tradition was to cry loudly and almost chant in a rhythmic manner. Paramedics were on hand to help those who fainted in the heat or from the intensity of the emotion. We had arranged to meet Michael's family at the spot. I knew his mother and sisters would be there. I did not expect his ex girlfriend.

When we arrived at the marker, his mother and his ex girlfriend were there. She had been the love of his life before me, and she was as beautiful as he had described her. She was taller than me, but dark, like me. She and I were meeting each other for the first time over Michael's grave. Unlike me, standing there in a numb state, she threw herself on the grave and kissed it, and wailed her grief. I watched her, fascinated, and felt a weird kind of competition for how we expressed ourselves. Did she love him more because she threw herself on the grave?

I embraced his mother and hugged her briefly. She and I had not been very close. I knew that Michael symbolized her husband, who had been killed in a motorcycle accident. Now, she had lost both husband and son. I tried to imagine myself on the back of Michael's motorcycle, where I had felt so free and so in love with both him and the country.

One day I was on the back of his motorcycle, or walking through the Bedouin market buying a week's supply of food, watching a sunset, lying in bed, and the next day he was gone.

A year later I watched myself on Israeli television embracing Michael's mother at the grave. My first response was how thin I was, how sculpted, and strange to myself. I watched the scene as if I were an actress in a film. I saw a thin, young, dark woman with my face, contorted in grief holding and hugging his mother: two women bound in their loss. It was almost as if the photographer had planned the pose and instructed us to embrace and cry at that precise moment.

I looked like I was grieving, yet I did not know how to grieve. From the moment I heard he was killed, I had a sense that I was in some kind of film following a script. Now, indeed, I was a character on the screen and had become the script.

It would take me many years to learn how to grieve, and even now, over thirty years later, I am not sure I know how.

I always seemed to cry on buses. It didn't matter what bus I was on, whether passing through the wealthy neighborhoods with large homes near Hebrew University, past the Parliament buildings, past the museums, or the green and brown hills that surrounded the city. It might be a religious neighborhood where men dressed in long black coats, black hats, and the women covered themselves modestly in long sleeved blouses, long skirts, and wore wigs or hats to cover their hair. Then I felt like I was in a ghetto in Eastern Europe at the beginning of the century, except for the Mediterranean sun and intense heat.

Nuns, monks, Arabs, Sufis, and Buddhists dressed in orange robes congregated in downtown Jerusalem in the crowds competing for God carving their own space in this blood drenched city full of history and culture. I loved it all: the smells, the spices, the marketplace, the Old City with winding streets and alleyways, and Arab shopkeepers shouting out bargains entreating tourists to come buy.

The problem was that I saw Michael everywhere. I felt robbed, and the loss hit me on buses for some reason. It was usually bus number five which made its way through the city, or bus number eighteen, which took me home from the university. Here, in my adopted city, my grief emerged. I often dreamed about calling Michael on the phone, but he would not answer. Sometimes, in these dreams, his mother would answer and say he could not come to the phone. She would inform me that he was out, or worse, dating another woman. Perhaps he had returned to his former love. Jealousy took over the grief. I woke up glad that he was not with another woman, relieved that he was dead.

Grief Times Two

He reached for
his duffel bag
grabbed his rifle
from the closet.

I wanted to walk him
to the road
but he said no.

Later, the soldiers
who had been with him
in the tank
told me his lungs
shattered
like a thousand pieces of glass.

Those clear blue eyes
closed as if asleep.
No sign of blood or injury.
His lungs
like the bomb that hit,
split into itself.

His former girlfriend
beat me to the grave,
She flung herself on the dirt
and wailed in rhythmic
ancient Hebrew fashion.

Still jealous of her beauty,
I just stood there,
watching.

The First Time: 1970

It seemed like the right time. It was 1970; I was turning nineteen, studying at Hebrew University in Jerusalem, in love with my boyfriend who lived in New York where he was finishing college. I wrote long passionate letters and made constant phone calls from Israel. I planned a trip back to see him. We had met during my senior year in high school, and only begun to explore our sexual relationship. Now was the time to lose my virginity, I decided, so before this critical initiation rite, I made an appointment to see a doctor at Haddassah Hospital about birth control.

Hadassah was situated above Ein-Karem, which was once a picturesque Arab village. The hospital loomed like a fortress in the Jerusalem hills. I took the bus, and like every time I took a bus in Jerusalem, I could not believe how dramatic the city appeared. No matter where I went, I felt like I was living out a biblical novel where the landscape had not changed. The smell of pines and eucalyptus lingered in the air, and the gold dome of the Temple of the Rock shimmered in the distance. I rode the bus with all kinds of people, from Orthodox Jews to sexily clad young women from soldiers with their rifles, to people carrying fruits and vegetables from the outdoor market.

I entered the young doctor's office with some trepidation since it was my first visit. It would become a familiar scene later on in my life as I would enter each gynecologist's office: certificates hung on the wall declaring the doctor's medical training, a table, and stirrups. I was unfamiliar with the protocol of waiting for the doctor with the flimsy sheet-like covering and had never seen stirrups before where I would lie wide open. I felt vulnerable and strangely sexual.

The doctor entered the room and sat silently at the edge of the table readying his instruments, saying nothing about what he was about to do or what I would feel. Seconds later, I felt an enormous stabbing pain and screamed out. I had never felt a pain like that before. I had no idea what had just happened, and concluded that it must be part of the exam. The doctor remained silent about my scream, as if it had not even occurred. He eventually told me to get up from the table. It was then I noticed blood on the floor. Blood was still running down my leg, as I reached for my pants and wiped it off with a paper towel, waiting for the doctor to explain what had happened. He said nothing, I looked at the blood that lay below me, still not fully comprehending that it was mine, and quickly got dressed. I just wanted to get out of there, and I forgot to ask about birth control. I wanted to return to the safety of my dorm room. I fled with the image of blood on the floor and a sore sensation between my legs.

The ride back on the bus did not seem romantic or dramatic; it felt like something terrible had happened. The grown-up pride of planning to lose my virginity was replaced with a kind of inexplicable shame and confusion. I kept seeing myself getting off the table, cleaning my leg, wondering about the blood on the floor.

A few months later, as I had planned when I made that terrible trip to Hadassah, I was in my New York boyfriend's parents' one bedroom apartment. His parents were elderly and had gone to bed early. We were to sleep in the living room, and I planned to lose my virginity on that couch. Instead of pills or a diaphragm, I bought a "sponge" at the local Walgreens. When I think back, I realize that this was not about the relationship, but more about what I visualized as a sexual gateway. The apartment was crowded and dusty and full of the years of living there. Jewish ritual objects were everywhere: a silver menorah, Sabbath candlesticks, old, musty pictures, and family photos. This was not how I had pictured losing my virginity; I had hoped for passion and romance and found myself in this inadequate setting. I inserted the sponge in his parents' bathroom amidst the family medications and a kind of musty smell.

I was self-conscious about having sex in the living room, where they might hear us. But since this was the only space we had, and he was so eager to "do it," and I was so determined to "lose it," I went along with the idea. After a few minutes and a groan or two from him, he rolled over towards the back of the small sofa. I thought I would feel something, some change, some climax. Where was that movie scene, breathtaking, noisy, mutual gratification?

Much like at Hadassah Hospital, I had no idea what had just happened. The doctor punctured me with a medical instrument; my boyfriend penetrated me with his penis. Both times I was ignorant.

Only later did it dawn on me I had lost my virginity twice: not only with my boyfriend in his parents' living room in New York, but also on the table at Hadassah Hospital by the doctor with a cold steel speculum. I had passively complied both times. I had kept quiet with the young doctor who had made a mistake and was not going to acknowledge my pain and loss, just as I had allowed myself to have sex in a place that did not seem right that gave me no pleasure. Hopeful pride was replaced twice with humiliation and shame.

What a way to begin my sexual journey. I wonder how many other women have had similar experiences and chosen to remain silent. I trusted both the doctor and my boyfriend to support me at a time of tremendous vulnerability. Instead, I felt violated and ignored.

The impersonal clinic and the crowded, dusty, living room crammed with memorabilia became one for me. The Jerusalem hills scented with pine and eucalyptus that I saw from my window on Bus Number 18 had transformed into the cold examination room at the Hadassah clinic, merging with the cramped, crowded apartment in New York where my boyfriend's parents lay sleeping a few yards away. I need only recall the strong ancient scent of the Judean hills to be that young woman who longed to grow up.

Tuna Fish Sandwiches: 2000

The first person I fell in love with was my mother. If I could choose a moment to relive, it would be walking back from school to have lunch every day with my mother in Newark, New Jersey. I immediately feel loved and safe when I think of the lunch my mother prepared for me every day from first grade through fifth grade. I would walk home from Chancellor Avenue School, that large, imposing structure, to our trim, green and white house on Fabian Place, near Summit Avenue. Growing up in the fifties meant walking home for lunch and then returning to school. It was a ritual that allowed me to connect with my mother and became a haven in the middle of the day. She always prepared the same sandwich: tuna fish with generous amounts of Hellmans mayonnaise, a squeeze of lemon, and lots of green onion).

Lunch was much more than food; it was time with my mother. After school she taught Hebrew at a local synagogue, and I missed her being home after school. At least in the middle of the day, she was waiting for me. No matter what happened to me that day: disappointments, a bad grade, taunts from a classmate, being "bullied" by one of the "bad" girls, the tuna fish sandwich was my comfort food and balanced the pain and torment of life in a an urban public school.

When my mother lay dying in the hospital in San Francisco, I could not easily accept her death. Before I visited her, I went to the hospital cafeteria to eat chocolate pudding: another childhood favorite and specialty of hers. She cooked it from a mix and boiled the pudding, thick and rich, deep in chocolate color and texture. I remember the burned aroma of chocolate, and the bubbles forming in the process. I could not find the tuna fish sandwiches, but the pudding was a good second choice to bring me back to the green and white house on Summit Avenue when life was fairly innocent and good, and my mother was young and healthy and waited for me every day.

I would do anything to have that sandwich back today and speak with my young and healthy mother with her jet black hair with white streaks, her clothes of vibrant colors, and her hugs and kisses. I just want to walk through that door once more and find her, see her smile, feel her love, hug her, and breathe her in. I even loved the ragged scar on her arm that she had gotten as a child in a terrible accident when she was twelve years old. She had run out into the street chased by a hive of bees, and her arm had got caught in a moving car door that dragged her down the street. She was self-conscious about the scar; it marred her beauty, or so she thought, yet it was a testament to her resilience. I could not imagine her without the scar.

Despite my fifty-nine year old body, I am still the daughter, the baby, the young woman, the new mother, the older mother, the adolescent. I am all those things, and the need for my mother does not diminish. I still want that tuna fish sandwich she prepared for me with lots of mayonnaise, some lemon and green onion on fresh rye bread. Even if I try to make the sandwich the same way, it can never come out the way my mother made it.

Rakafot (Cyclamen)

Safeway sells your favorite flowers
Those purple and red ones
that cover the Israeli hills and fields.
The woman behind the counter
tells me they are perfect for graves.

I met a student of yours today.
What she remembered most
was the fantastic jewelry you wore:
bright, flamboyant, exotic,
chunks of silver or gold
reds and greens.

And then there was that
one silver streak in
your jet black hair
and your thick accent.

Today I placed
the purple and red
cyclamen, rakafot,
on that dark, grey stone
like fantastic jewelry.

Red High Heels: 1961

We ran away at Halloween when we were eleven years old. Stephanie had decided that we could not just do the usual trick or treating in our two safe streets in Newark. We had to go "beyond" the neighborhood to somewhere unfamiliar. The well ordered streets of Newark turned into streets with large apartment buildings where it was not possible to knock on the door and chant our usual "trick or treat." These streets were more imposing, closer to the center of town, where there was more traffic and department stores like Woolworths. I prayed my parents would not worry or find out that we had broken away from Grumman Avenue, where we both lived.

We dressed in sexy tight fighting clothes. I usually wore baggy, muted shirts which would become my uniform as I got older and as my breasts developed. Stephanie burst out of everything. Her breasts bulged, her thighs were perfectly sculpted, and she enjoyed showing off her body. She was one of the few eleven year old girls who actually had cleavage to show. Boys loved her. She was a risk taker, a seeker; I was the intellectual, the critic, and I was fearful. I was infatuated with her and her chain smoking mother who wore equally sexy clothes, had bleached blonde hair, and spoke in a sultry, sexy, smoker's voice.

I was always "hiding" my full size breasts, yet with Stephanie I dared to wear the kind of clothes that were more her style than mine. We wove our way through the streets of Newark in our red high heels and over the top, sophisticated, much too adult kind of clothes in search of adventure.

It was the first time I felt sexy and aware of my body, and it was only because of Stephanie that I dared exit my safety zone. We were not only exiting our safe, well known Newark neighborhood, but venturing forth into a more flirtatious adult world. We were budding women in our eleven year old bodies.

I envied her body: her calves were well developed and seemed to bulge with muscle and she knew how to reveal cleavage. Stephanie was part "shiksa," (Yiddish for not Jewish) since her mother was not Jewish, and while many of us in Newark were darker, and less svelte; her blonde hair and sexy body seemed more exotic than the rest of us. The risk I took with her that Halloween signaled the change in Newark. It was on the verge of exploding into violence. It was as if our changing bodies and the turbulence of adolescence mirrored the riots that would soon take place and change Newark and other cities forever. Fires were set throughout the city by some members of the black community in one of the infamous "riots" that swept the nation pre-1967.

Before the 1967 riots, Newark was a middle class Jewish city that appeared ordinary. I found refuge in our green and white house on Grumman Avenue, playing in the street with neighborhood kids. I felt safe in the elementary school on the main street which took up half the block. I knew every teacher by name. I especially remembered my kindergarten teacher, Mrs. Novack, with her steel rimmed glasses and kind voice. Her daily snacks of graham crackers and milk, and naps that followed, had been a cocoon before the days when children would experience kindergarten as a pressure ridden class that decided the rest of their academic future. In those days, we were still allowed to look forward to graham crackers and milk and to our naps.

It felt deliciously taboo to follow Stephanie in her red high heels, blond hair, and sexy clothes with me in pursuit. I would have followed her anywhere.

I have no memory of those streets, or how long we were away, or if my parents worried and if there were any consequences for our actions. As an eleven year old, I dared to dream of being out of the box while struggling for my need for safety. At the same time I yearned for adventure.

Stephanie became my mentor for a window into a world I was desperately curious about but not ready to enter. It made sense, then, that she would designate me as a "timekeeper" for her and her boyfriend while they made out. Sex is not always about having sex: it is about a feeling, a moment, a turning point, a visual. That moment, sitting a few feet away from Stephanie and her boyfriend on a roof as the evening turned dark and our parents had not called us to dinner yet, was an erotic moment. I can still feel the summer breeze as they kissed in the twilight as I "kept time."

Stephanie and I lost touch after I moved from Newark to the suburbs. I moved to a street named "Pleasant Valley Way," and the neat homes and basketball courts with well trimmed lawns replaced the urban gritty streets of Newark. Later, I heard that she became a teenage mother at seventeen. She married her boyfriend and had a son. I wondered how she felt about it: being a single teenage mother in the sixties was still fairly outrageous and unconventional. I wanted to talk to her, to ask her how it all worked out. I wonder if she wanted to be me as much as I wanted to be her.

A Black and White Photo: 1960

There we are: my brother at five up to my shoulder, dressed in a traditional Dutchman's costume with a cigarette in his mouth and one hand in his pocket, and me at nine in a traditional female version of the Dutchwoman: white kerchief on my head, white apron and bib over a long black dress. I'm holding on to a wooden spinning wheel, and in the background there are old fashioned wicker chairs and elegant formal wallpaper, with Dutch blue plates adorning the shelf behind us. I smile slightly for the camera; my brother is a bit more serious. We could be old fashioned Dutch children, but look a bit too Semitic. We are both dark-skinned, with big brown eyes--two Jewish children in 1960 posing as Dutch children in a country still suffering the devastating after effects of World War II. We are in Rotterdam, a bombed out city, trying to rebuild itself from the ashes of the war. My father seemed to be trying to recover his lost childhood by returning to Europe and seeking the sensations, the smells, the food, and the images he left behind. Was this photograph a way for him to play out a fantasy of belonging? Instead of being the fearful refugee child, he could have us pose as traditional Dutch children who belonged to their culture, their language, and their history.

My brother and I became these posed characters in an alien setting, like my father, trying to find our place in the world. Since Rotterdam had been so heavily bombed, everything seemed newly replaced. They built new malls, new shops, new houses, new gardens, and new parks. Holland smelled of rain, either impending or just finished. It was gray and rainy, but charming in so many ways and a sanctuary for my family, away from grimy, industrial Newark, New Jersey. Here, we could feed ducks in ponds and drink cups of hot chocolate. Rotterdam always sparkled. Flowers were everywhere: purple or yellow tulips or red geraniums. We didn't have to worry about crime or race riots or what neighborhood we found ourselves in. In that photograph, my brother and I could pretend we were Dutch. We could forget about feeling different. We could forget our history of fleeing the Nazis and the relatives killed in concentration camps. It was in Holland I discovered A. E. Milne's *Winnie the Pooh,* since it was the only English language book in the Dutch library. I must have read that book a hundred times, nearly memorizing it. While I was fascinated by the guttural sounds of Dutch, I could not understand or read it. I yearned to read anything in English. Language seemed to be my home, no matter where I was, even at nine. I did not belong to New Jersey, either. I wanted to be like my Christian friends who celebrated Christmas, got presents, and ice skated gracefully in the park. My name was different, I looked different, and I desperately wanted to be blonde and mainstream.

I look at that photograph now, and I recognize that my brother and I don't really belong in the picture, though it has become a memory of the two of us. We don't have many photographs of us together. We never discussed taking it or how we felt when we did. I don't remember much about our early relationship. I don't know what we did that day, or what we said to one another, or how we felt, dressed up in a strange outfit. I do know that we inherited from our father, who never seemed to find it, the trait of constantly looking for our place.

Shopping on Shenkin Street: 2006

Shenkin Street had become chic, like the East Village in New York or Union Street in San Francisco. It was a far cry from what I remembered during my childhood visits to Israel, when this street was shabby and worn, where apartment buildings had bullet holes from various wars, and small shops were owned by quiet European Jewish immigrants. "Shenkin Street," now sold everything from freshly squeezed carrot juice to computers, the latest fashions, jewelry, souvenirs, and modern Israeli art. The crowd that strolled up and down Shenkin was hip and young. It was full of tourists, as well as, ordinary Israelis who lived in the area or who came to shop and be part of this trendy Tel-Aviv neighborhood.

I walked with Dina, my young friend who wore hip hugger pants, a short tank top that showed off her flat belly, and red curly hair which came down past her shoulders. Our relationship was somewhere between equals and mother-daughter. Our age difference showed when I tried to keep up with Dina's energy, and this day was no exception. We had met in New York at an educators' conference and now, when I came to visit Israel, Dina promised to show me around Tel-Aviv. Shenkin Street was our first stop.

Dina suddenly pulled me into a store. There was no name on the front. It was hard to determine what the store sold: clothes, gifts, or lingerie. I thought it was strange that there was no name.

"Here, you need to shop in this store. I bought something here a few months ago. Of course, I haven't used it yet," she laughed nervously.

A young woman behind the counter seemed even younger than Dina, with long black hair, no make-up, double pierced ears, and multiple tattoos. She probably weighed no more than ninety pounds.

"Do you ladies want my introductory lecture?"

I realized we were in a sex shop, and while discreet, it displayed vibrators in the form of giant penises. What would it be like, I wondered, to pull that out of a drawer, or God forbid, have airport security pull it out of my suitcase.

We were the only customers in the shop, and I thought about the glaring newspaper headlines that morning about Gilad Shalit, a nineteen year-old soldier, kidnapped in Gaza by Hamas. The fate of his two fellow soldiers was still unknown. Gilad's photo appeared in every newspaper, his adolescent face and large glasses making him look more like a computer geek than a macho soldier. Perhaps he was neither. He did not seem to have the sculpted body, scruffy beard, or rugged features of a typical soldier. He was fresh, young, innocent, and his eyes behind those glasses could not have suspected that he might be kidnapped by terrorists. Gilad seemed like he belonged in a college classroom behind a desk, not a hostage in a two thousand year old battle.

My youngest son was twenty-one, two years older than Gilad, and in his third year of college. I tried to connect the headlines, Gilad's face, my own son's face, and the young woman's sales pitch.

"Just remember, "she said, "these vibrators can provide you with many orgasms. Why be satisfied with one or none when you can have several?" She began to demonstrate the qualities of the vibrators on Dina's arm

"Here is one of our favorites, called the butterfly," she said with a gentle whiz motion.

Dina seemed more at home in this store than me. Was the younger generation more comfortable with the technology of sex? The sales clerk spoke about orgasms as naturally as if she were selling music or any item for that matter. It could have been jeans, perfume, or a new necklace. Where was the intimacy and the passion associated with sex? During the seventies, when I came of age, women were not afraid to talk about sex, but this seemed different. This young woman seemed to talk about sexual props with almost a religious fervor, and she began to compare the virtues of the clitoral orgasm to the vaginal orgasm.

It was surreal: a young soldier my son's age had been kidnapped, and here we were: three women, one in her fifties, one in her twenties, with an even younger sales clerk, promoting orgasms in a sex store. That could not have happened during my childhood when during summers when visiting my grandmother, I had walked these streets to her favorite library to borrow books, or to the local butcher to buy meat for dinner. I suddenly wanted to leave the store; I tried to forget this new modern Shenkin and remember the older, more intimate street that was historic and quaint.

I said, "Let's get out of here. It feels like I can't breathe, and I am not interested in buying any of these things."

We exited to the nearby "shuk," an open market that sold pitas, olives, fruit, and vegetables. With its earthy smells and the shouts of shopkeepers, the market contrasted the fashionable Shenkin.

As we sat in the shade with an ice-cold orange soda, I began to think about how much I had loved this country. I had left Israel in 1976, three years after the Yom Kippur War, after my fiancé had been killed. It had become too difficult to live in this turbulent country where war and sex, religion and passion, guns and books, lived side by side. I sought refuge in San Francisco, the "City of Love," which was about hippies, flowers and peace, not about war and death. It had been my haven for thirty years and now on this hot, summer day, the reality of war screamed once more in the headlines.

I remembered Shenkin Street during the Yom Kippur War of 1973: it was empty and silent, part of a ghost town with curfews. I had walked up and down this street at the age of twenty-two bargaining with God for my Michael to be simply wounded, but not to die. Just let him return, I had pleaded. He was killed the first week of the war in the desert. God had not listened.

Dina's reality was different. Even though she had grown up in Israel, she sought excitement, dates on the Internet, or world travel. She had not lived through any wars; even though she lived with the constant tension war creates. Right now, all Dina wanted was that I have fun, try on clothes, gossip, and be young. All I could do in this moment was remember thirty years back, riding on Michael's motorcycle and watching Jerusalem's hills fade into the sunset. After Michael's death, I still loved Israel but could not stay there without him. For me, the country and my fiancé were intertwined; one could not exist without the other. Shenkin Street was an old street in a new era, and the bullet ridden apartment buildings were now condominiums. I would try to forget about Gilad Shalit's parents, my own son who could have been Gilad, or

Michael's killed over thirty years ago. I would try to live in the present, on a shopping spree in Tel-Aviv, with my young, attractive friend, to what appeared to be a different Israel.

I knew it was impossible to do that; I could not forget my past in this country. Shenkin Street might have changed, and Israel had as well in many ways, but it was always a country at war, a country where parents never knew if their sons or daughters would return home safely, or at all. Shopping on this street allowed me to evade that reality for just a bit longer, and to remember myself, a younger woman, in love, holding tightly on to her fiancé from the back of a motorcycle as Jerusalem was bathed in pink and gold. Shenkin Street was not the same anymore; like Michael, it remained a memory.

Four Women at "The Grand Piano": 1979

We decided to meet at our favorite café in Haight Ashbury. My friends and I loved this place: somewhat sleazy, hippy dippy, trying to be or still is the typical Haight coffee house: long haired men, jeans, beards, smells of soup, strong coffee, or spaghetti. Punk rockers sat nearby with red and orange hair, earrings in their noses and ears, speaking about betrayal with enthusiasm, while conversations floated all around us: "I work at the Bay, oh, and then you must know...." He is such a shit...I couldn't believe it...."A dark, gentle looking man was reading the newspaper at the table nearby. It was a gray and foggy morning in San Francisco in the late seventies. We chose this place to gossip, try to articulate our dilemmas, see if we could create a writer's group, and try to make sense of our realities with conversation and coffee.

Barbara walked in just as this guy at the next table and I were discussing the bad light. I felt his loneliness, the way he was kind of coming on to me, and wondered if I wanted to know him. No, not now. I didn't want to know some strange, needy, unknown man. I turned my attention to Barbara, who was the first of the three friends to arrive.

Barbara and I met at San Francisco State University, where we were both enrolled in a master's program in literature. One day, when a class was cancelled, we decided to take sandwiches into an empty classroom, and while we munched, we ended up revealing our innermost secrets and desires: her breakdown, my despair over Michael's death, our conflicts in relationships, existential questions like did love and freedom ever mix? In conversation, Barbara became the dynamic, caustic, brilliant woman she was. Intellectually driven, she seemed to write flawlessly and get A's on her papers. She was very different than what she appeared to be: a quiet, unassertive, pale blonde who hid in various turtlenecks. What stood out from our many conversations were her broken dreams and her anger at an alcoholic mother.

"What I wanted most," Barbara told me, "my mother never gave me, and now it is too late. I wanted an academic education; my life would be different now if I already had it and didn't have to work so hard to get it. I am tired of always working, always juggling things in my life."

I realized how hard it was for her to work and go to school, to heal from an abusive marriage, to struggle with all those parts of her life, always under the shadow of an alcoholic mother who she had to constantly take care of. She could not yet free herself of her mother's oppressive presence. In some ways, her mother's spirit joined us at that table at the Grand Piano. Despite her mother's destructive influence, I knew that Barbara would be our guiding force, the calm, organized one who would help us gather our thoughts and help make our writing into something cohesive.

I miss Barbara. She recently died from cancer, and I know that I won't find another friend who loved me like she did, who knew how to be calm in the face of emotional fire.

The next person to enter the café was Adrian. She was from Israel and had lived in San Francisco for four years. Adrian had recently exited from a marriage. She had never written her own checks; her critical husband robbed her of confidence and filled her with resentment. She seemed to flower outside her marriage. Adrian wore sexy tight clothes, high heels, bright colors, flashy earrings, and she had recently fallen in love with a British man who constantly told her how great she was. He did not criticize her constantly or belittle her. She had begun to find herself. Adrian and I had also met at the university and realized that we had both been part of each other's past in Israel.

A story I had written about Michael's life linked us. I had nonchalantly decided to share it with Adrian one day after class, over coffee. I happened to have it in my bag and asked her if she wanted to read it. In an emotional moment after reading the story, Adrian asked me if my story was true. I answered that it was, and in between her tears, she told me she knew Michael. He lived across the street from her and had often confided in her about his relationship with me. He told her that he sensed she would like me and that we could be friends. But we never met in Israel. He was killed before that meeting took place. It would take a class at San Francisco State University to find each other, and the crumpled story in my bag.

We remained close friends for the next thirty years. But at that moment, we had just begun the friendship, and I forever see her in her sexy outfits, her high heels, her dyed hair, and her need to be free of her marriage. She brought the spirit of my dead fiancé to the group, along with the memory of the Israeli desert.

The last to enter the café was Lydia, a black poet and mother of an eleven year old girl. Lydia was passionate and outspoken and had short cropped hair and wore colorful clothes. She had a deep, resonant voice. She often shared her poetry with us in our poetry class, and I was taken with her voice, her passions, her poetry, while being a young mother at twenty-eight, to an adolescent daughter. Lydia was somewhat suspicious of us: newer to the group, struggling with her poetry while at the same time working full time and supporting her daughter. I was somewhat infatuated with her. She had inspired me to write a poem in her honor and I was looking forward to sharing it with the group, though also nervous about her reaction. She brought the spirit of single motherhood and poetry to the table at The Grand Piano.

I looked around the table. All these women were part of me: Barbara, Adrian, and Lydia. All of us were struggling to express ourselves and liberate ourselves from broken dreams and the people in our lives who held us back: our mothers, lovers, and husbands. I wanted to tell Barbara: get your Ph.D, and don't let your mother stand in your way. Adrian: free yourself of your marriage and blossom in a new way. Lydia: you can be both mother and poet. As for me: Let go of the Israeli dream of my lover killed near a tank, try to be a writer and actress, become a mother and wife, continue to be perpetual lover, observer, friend.

Our reality was San Francisco in 1979. What did we need to let go of, and what did we try to embrace? One thing was certain: we had each other for the moment at this café in the Haight Ashbury sitting round the table at The Grand Piano figuring out the melody of our lives.

I miss Barbara who died, Adrian who moved to New York, Lydia, whom I never saw again, and the parts of me who never became what I hoped.

The Sukkah

Sweet smelling etrog
ancient fruit
citrus perfumed
breathe it in and return to the wilderness
where Hebrews wandered
and built these booths.

Long elegant palm leaves
hover above us
revealing bits of sky
so God can peek in.

Shake the palm in six directions
first towards Jerusalem
and then west north south
upwards and down
to all the peoples of the Middle East,
Jews, Palestinians, Bedouins, Druze,
Christians, Greek and Russian Orthodox.

We eat and sleep in the Sukkah,
a hut made out of wood
with branches for a roof,
as our forefathers and foremothers.
I feel the breeze from the hot dry desert.
A hard rain drenches the Sukkah.

On this holiday of harvest and temporary shelter
we remember
the homeless and those
who lost their homes to war and to battles,

who were displaced and sometimes forgotten,
to those who choose to wander
and to those who are forced to

I remember the Israeli desert
the orange and red sunsets,
swish of the water sprinklers,
the roads that seemed to lead to nowhere.
Only the Bedouins know where to go
in the curves of the vast desert.

I still feel
the desert wind on my face
on the back of a motorcycle
riding away from the city
towards the palm laden, temporary Sukkot booths in autumn
ancient and new country.
The temporary booths of Sukkot
Remind me of temporary graves
Rows and rows of identical gravesones
marked not by name, but by number.
I searched for the one that was my lover.
I was 22.
He was 24.

I close my eyes and
smell the sage and brush.
mourn the freedom
and possibility that ended
before Sukkot.

Shake the Hadas,
the myrtle leaf
to the East,
to Jerusalem, to all the
directions of the world,
to the desert,
to my people,
to peace.

In Labor: 1983

I squatted on the floor as the labor nurse instructed and thought to myself, I can't believe women go through this every day, every minute, through the centuries. My insides were being sucked out, and the earth felt like it was opening beneath me and I would be swallowed up, or I would have the worst case of diarrhea ever. This was the "natural" act of labor, of giving birth, that many women could not wait to experience. I just wanted it over with. I had dreaded this moment since I found out I was pregnant. I had actually loved the feeling of pregnancy; I lay on my sofa feeling the baby's movements inside me and following that last fist or kick as a spot on my belly tightened. I enjoyed the anticipation of pregnancy itself, but did not look forward to the delivery. Why didn't women talk about this? If they did, would nobody get pregnant?

In the spirit of "political correctness" during the early eighties, we had signed up for the Alternative Birth Center in the hospital which served as the antithesis of the traditional, sterile, cold, impersonal space. Here was a cozy kind of bedroom with personal furnishings that were to remind us of our home, designed to minimize the impersonal mode of that outdated, style of giving birth. I desperately wanted the "other" politically "incorrect" style that my mother had in the 1950's. Just put me out and bring back the clean baby, and let me know about it afterwards! I had enough of the squatting, the walking, the nurse telling me to have Ofer, my husband, stimulate my nipples! After hours of trying to give birth naturally, the doctor decided I was not able to dilate, so she gave me pitocin to stimulate labor hurry it along. This was another form of torture: intense contractions that led to nowhere. I lay on the table and dreaded each one. Every contraction promised redemption. I would open up; my baby would come out. But this did not work.

Finally, it was decided I would have to have a C-section. As I was wheeled into the operating room, I began to shake uncontrollably. I remembered being five years old and having my tonsils out. Then, too, I shook like a leaf when I saw the table, the instruments, the masked staff, and the bright lights. I was back to being five, only I was thirty-two about to give birth to a baby boy. I felt as alone and scared as I had at five. Instead of becoming a mother, I wanted my own mother to hold me and assure me that this would be alright. The doctors had to hold me down in order to give me the epidural so that my shaking would not impede the sedation.

After a few minutes of listening to the doctors talk about my blood spurting out, I felt a "whoosh" as my son was vacuumed out of me. The lack of pain was a relief. Letting others do the work of giving birth seemed like a gift, yet the actual moment of birth seemed like it belonged to someone else. Not me. I was removed from myself, an object on a table being discussed with blood spurting. My body was sedated, my baby was pulled out from inside, and were sewn back. I was not able to meet my son who had just emerged. I wasn't able to hold him or see him. He had trouble breathing and needed to be whisked away to the intensive care nursery.

It would take time to bond with him, to adjust to being a mother, and it would take more time the next time I gave birth. Now my two sons mean more than anything to me; I would walk through fire to rescue them if needed. Then, I was just learning how to be a mother.

A Hospital Note: 1995

I stood at the nurse's station when I overheard the conversation about my mother between her social worker and the nurse.

"So, how's Mrs. Blutinger? Are we transferring her anywhere?"

The social worker laughed, "Oh, no, Mrs. Blutinger isn't going anywhere."

That conversation was the first in a series of indignities and violations that marked my mother's last week of life at this prestigious hospital. The same social worker who laughed about my "mother not going anywhere," had spoken to me about hospice options two days earlier after my mother's condition deteriorated from chronic illness to terminal. I asked the social worker to wait until I spoke to my mother. She had tried to cover up her illness for two decades, and now that she was approaching death, I wasn't sure she had given up on the denial. Or was it my own denial? I could not imagine life without her. Ever since I was a child, the worst thing I could think of was her death. I had no idea how to live without her. The next morning as I helped feed my mother breakfast, the social worker walked in with forms for her to sign. I took the papers from her hand and read: *I have less than six months to live and agree to the conditions of hospice care.* How could I let her sign that form without any preparation? I had not been given time to speak to her. I was grateful that I was in the room, and she was not alone when the social worker entered. Time was a commodity here; it was all about negotiating how to preserve it and how to find the right moment to speak about things we never dared speak about before. I vowed to find the right moment to speak to my mother. It turned out I would not find that moment.

I arrived early the next morning to find a note on my mother's closed door. It read: "Please see the nurse." Confused, I went to the nurse's station, to find my father slumped in a chair nearby, a vacant expression on his face. "She's gone," he told me.

I stared back at the door. Behind it was my mother. Now I understood the significance of the note. I felt like I had been hit in the stomach as I realized that behind the door, my mother lay dead.

Later, we discovered she had died four hours before we arrived at the hospital. No one had called us. There had been some kind of confusion as to who would notify us. I thought about how that note signified the end of my mother's life, a life of drama and emotions, events and children, suffering and hope, her life of wandering between two countries and never really finding her home, following me and my family halfway around the world. She was my best friend and in her death, she was condensed to a note with instructions to see a nurse.

The morning at the hospital began with the note and ended with the chaplain's suggestion I say farewell to my mother. I imagined a peaceful scene where I would gently plant a kiss on her forehead, and perhaps find some solace in that moment. Instead what greeted me was a skeletal figure of my mother, her mouth wide open, her eyes staring ahead. I looked and backed out of the room quickly: here was her final indignity. The nurses had not prepared her body. Why had no one bothered to take care of her, to close her eyes and her mouth? Why had the chaplain not checked her condition before he thought of asking me to enter her room?

Life begins and ends in hospitals and everyday dramas are played out, perhaps similar to my mother's. I needed to embark on my own investigation about how and when she died. I had to ask and wonder if she was regularly checked and what the exact time of death was. I had to request her medical records, which arrived weeks later with many unanswered questions. The medical records did not explain the lack of notification or why she was left unattended after her death. I did not want just an apology; I wanted an explanation. I wanted to personally speak to her doctor whom she had trusted and seen for years, who did not call us that night, but spoke to us only very briefly that morning. I felt betrayed by a system that exhibited very little compassion or dignity towards my mother as a patient and to us as a family.

As I look back, I remember the social worker laughing with the nurse, not knowing I was nearby. I think of my mother signing forms which would have further demoralized her, of her curt and distant doctor, of my father's shell shocked expression as he sat in one of the lobby chairs. I think of what I saw when I entered her room to say a final farewell.

I try to forget the last image I had of her, but it often comes to me in my dreams. I still miss her fifteen years later and think of her every day. In my imagination, I place the kiss on her forehead, hold her hand, and tell her how much I love her. I hope she knows.

I Loved Your Scar

I loved your scar
the way it stretched across your arm
in slipshod fashion. A zigzag
of flesh colored patches creating their own design
branding your moment of adolescent terror.

A young girl in Palestine 1939
shiny, jet black hair
sculpted face.
Even then, you resembled Merle Oberon,
the famous actress.

You were always beautiful.

I was fourteen when we walked the streets of Tel-Aviv
and you told me of the fear that drove you out
not looking, frantic,
the ominous sound of the bees
chasing you and others—
a hive gone wild.

In those early days
not that many cars
a few palm trees
thick stone apartment buildings
sandy lots
some restaurants.
This was before the walking wounded
from the concentration camps
arrived
in a city that was not yet a city

a country not yet a country.

You were just beginning to find yourself
when you ran and a speeding car
caught your arm and held it tight
like someone savoring a meal, reluctant to let go of that last
morsel.
The driver continued dragging you through the street

You almost lost your arm,
but the doctors managed to save it
and give you the scar that would follow you through life—
revealing itself in sleeveless dresses
a bathing suit
or in your bra and underwear.

A tribute to your adolescent fear and triumph

I loved your scar.
It made you special.
Set you apart from other mothers.

I wanted to caress it,
to kiss it.
I stroked your scar when you lay dying in the hospital

I wanted to hold you in my arms and somehow
prevent you from dying.

Today I still want to kiss your scar
to remind me of when we walked the streets of Tel-Aviv
and you spoke about your childhood
of memory and longing
of mother and daughter
united by our love and our wounds.

I Remember the Ocean: 2004

I had a restless sleep, somewhat guilty that I had not responded to my father's frantic request the night before. He had called that Friday evening, his voice urgent and angry: "Why haven't you brought me my passport? You know I have a flight tonight at 7:00, and I won't make it to the airport if you don't bring it to me right now." How to interpret this latest demand? I had just placed him in a convalescent home three weeks ago, much against his will, and I hoped that he would adjust to this European style home where the atmosphere might remind him of Europe that he loved so much. He lived to travel, and after my mother died, it was his escape, his *raison d'être*. But he had become an invalid, and the only traveling he did was from his chair to his bed. He needed constant help, and he could no longer live in his apartment even with the twenty four hour help I had provided for him for the past year and a half. I knew this latest request seemed to indicate a decline, for there was no trip. The passport was symbolic both of his desire to travel and of his inability to do so.

"How about if I bring it to you tomorrow morning? I checked your ticket, Dad, and your flight is really not till tomorrow. I promise to bring it to you first thing in the morning."

He seemed to relax, and asked again if I was sure his flight was for the next day, and in my fatigue and not wanting to go there that evening and deal with his irrationality, I assured him it was for the next day. I braced myself when I went to sleep that night for whatever waited the next day.

That morning at 6:30 AM. the phone rang, and it was the hospital telling me that my father had been brought there and was unconscious and probably would not live more than the next forty-eight hours. The image of his passport flashed before me: should I have brought it? I might have seen him conscious and helped him play out his last travel fantasy: the one that had dominated his life. All our lives, he had traveled with us, or with my mother, or on his own. His favorite destination was Germany, his birthplace, and it was there that he thought he was going that night.

I went to the hospital to see him and he struggled to breathe, wrestling with life and with death. I could not bear to watch. I held his hand and told him I was there and hoped the doctors had been wrong. Perhaps he would live on for awhile. He had conquered death before, and I had been warned a few years ago that he would not survive. Was this another one of those times? I didn't think so. I had resisted the idea of his dying each time. We were not close and he repulsed me in many ways: his decline, his overweight body, his obsession with women and pornography, his lack of interest in my life and in the lives of his grandsons. Still, he was all I had left. If he died, I would be an orphan and who else could I talk to about my mother, whom I missed desperately? My childhood seemed to live on if he did. I tried to focus on pleasant memories.

The most vivid memory I had of me and my father was when we swam in the ocean in Israel. The water was always warm and soothing, and I rode on his back. We were one, and it was sensual and magical. He was strong and able and loving, and the water carried us so easily; the sun shone, the water sparkled. We were both young, and he was my daddy who could do no wrong. He was not the aging, helpless man who could no longer leave his apartment. And I was not responsible for his care, his spirit, and always depressed by his lack of energy, his lack of interest. He seemed only to come alive when I paid bills and took care of financial matters. I wished we could be back in the sea, father and daughter swimming—my handsome father.

I left the hospital and walked by the Pacific Ocean and cried at the thought of losing him. I walked and cried and did not want to face another death. This was all so hard.

The next morning the phone rang again: this time to tell me he had passed away during the night. Those phone calls are always so final, yet so unreal. I went to the hospital and saw his feet sticking out of the blankets. That would be my image of death. I stood in the room and tried to say good bye without seeing him. Only his feet were in sight; everything else was covered up.

I cried for us, for all the things we could not say to one another, for all the unexpressed love and unmet expectations, for the depression and sadness, for not bringing him the passport, for him wanting it so badly. I tried to say, Shalom, Abba, I will swim with you again, sometime. We will swim in the sea and I will hold on to your back, and you will be the father I always wanted.

The Passport: 2004

My father had many names. He was born Siegfried in Berlin in 1925, an only child to parents, William, born in Poland, and Adela, born in Vienna. My father escaped the beginning of Nazi Germany in 1933. William, my grandfather, had been arrested because he was a photographer, and the Nazis were suspicious of photographers. After a night in jail, William emerged, determined to get his family out of Germany. He needed no more signs that Germany was no longer a place for Jews. But leaving Germany was difficult for my father, because it was almost like a Garden of Eden for him. He was a happy child living in the exciting city of Berlin, and he never got over his exile. He always longed for German food, enjoyed speaking German, and made numerous trips back to visit. It was as if those eight years were frozen in time for little Siegfried, who clung to his mother on the train to Holland and then on the ship to Palestine. Of course, leaving Germany saved their lives.

Siegfried became Israel or "Yisrael" in Hebrew. In many ways he blossomed in the hot, dry climate of Israel and in the new city of Tel-Aviv. He became a muscular, good looking hunk, surrounded by women on the beaches of Tel-Aviv, and somewhere in that crowd, he met my mother. Yisrael was a jeweler by trade, but he felt claustrophobic sitting in that confined cubby peering over minute pieces of gold and silver. My parents, giving in to a mutual restless spirit, decided to leave for the United States. They made a striking couple, my mother dramatically exotic with thick black hair comparable to the movie actress of the day, Merle Oberon. My father had that body builder physique and classic good looks, and at twenty one and twenty two, respectively, they made their way to New York City.

Yisrael found his true identity in New Jersey where they settled, and where my brother and I were born. He was no longer the little boy, Siegfried, who reluctantly left Germany, who had become Yisrael who chose to leave Israel. He was now christened by his American business partner as "Sam." Now he was the fast-talking car salesman in Morristown, New Jersey, part owner of the first Volkswagen car agency, aptly named "The Little Car Company." No longer the displaced refugee, the jeweler or beach muscle man, he found us all a home, and worked his way into the American Dream.

Whether he was Siegfried, Yisrael, or Sam, the name I used for him throughout the years was "Pop." Many years later, after my mother died and he had once more left Israel to return to the States and to San Francisco where I lived, his restless spirit never left him; even on that last evening when he called me with a urgent request to bring him his passport so that he could return to Germany. He was convinced he had a flight the next morning. He had always been in love with Germany ever since he was forced to leave at eight years old. Now at almost eighty he still wanted to return. I told him I would bring him his passport the next morning. But he died before I could get there.

I said good-bye to Siegfried, the little German boy who never grew up and always wanted to return to his Germany; to Yisrael, the Israeli idealist who could not accept a new reality in Israel; to Sam who lived out the American dream, but never really seemed content. I wondered if he was happiest, perhaps, in Morristown, New Jersey, as the car salesman of his empire, "The Little Car Company," laughing with customers, and watching me watch him from the corner of the showroom, or maybe he was happiest when we swam in the ocean. I stood there at the edge of his bed in the hospital and thought of us in those warm, calm waters, so far from this moment.

A Pilgrimage: 1995

I get on a small wooden chair outside this simple cottage near Taos, New Mexico, and tried to look inside to learn more about D. H. Lawrence's life. The cottage was closed to visitors, but I was determined to get a glimpse of the interior. I hoped I wouldn't be accused of loitering or trespassing, but nothing stopped me. On the wall of the cottage were paintings done by Lawrence, and I was able to see some of the erotic portraits of men and women signed "Lorenzo." It was one of those moments you record in your head: the moment I stood on a bench in the oppressive heat of New Mexico looking into a window where this famous author had painted and lived. I could almost imagine him and Frieda talking, working, as I breathed in their past life.

I had reached the Lawrence Ranch that morning. As my roommate and I drove up the winding road which led to the ranch, I smelled eucalyptus and pine and thought of Jerusalem and the Israeli desert. My past was catching up to me in this brilliant New Mexico light. The ranch was rustic and did not look very different than it did in 1924 when D. H. Lawrence and his wife, Frieda, settled there. The cabin they lived in was a simple building, and the path behind it led to a series of steps to the white shrine with a phoenix, a symbol of renewal in Lawrence's work, was sitting up on the front roof. The large initials DHL were carved into the concrete.

Once inside the shrine is a sign-in guest register to the left. People had signed their names and written personally to D. H. Lawrence. I wrote: "I am with you, D. H., asking, experiencing, wondering, questing, dreaming, and loving." I could see what drew Lawrence to this place. New Mexico with its golden light, the scent of pine trees, starry, clear nights and a bright white moon, all reflected his love for life even as he wrote about characters in gray, gloomy England. I loved Lawrence for the way he wrote about women: they were strong, sexual characters who were not afraid to fulfill their innermost desires.

The first time I saw some of D. H. Lawrence's paintings was in Taos at the La Fonda De Taos Inn when the owner, Saki, invited me to his room. Saki was a famous character of Taos, nicknamed the "Don Juan of Taos," and he had mixed with the famous, the rich and the literary, old time Taos artists, movie stars, foreign diplomats, and local and international friends who had all congregated at this hotel painted in shades of blue. My room at La Fonda was painted blue; the walls of the lobby were blue in stark contrast to the intense gold and brown of the desert surrounding Taos. Saki, true to his nickname, made a habit of inviting young women to his room. I was no exception, and I sat in his cluttered room full of portraits, paintings, shelves of books, and knick knacks. He showed me dusty D. H. Lawrence novels signed by Frieda and dedicated to Saki; he told me that he and Picasso had shared a certain Swedish lover. Saki invited my roommate and me to swim with him that night at one of his friend's homes. We agreed to meet and drive with him to the home outside Taos.

It was a magical evening. Either no one lived at this house or they were gone. We swam in the pool on a dark night illuminated by the moon and millions of stars. Saki spoke to us about the old days and the home of some long forgotten movie star as we swam. It was another one of those moments I would record, along with looking into the window of the cottage and seeing D. H. Lawrence paintings. New Mexico was about nature and sky and colors and art and artists and writers and spirits of the past. It was about my own erotic longing and fantasies of becoming a writer, while being a mother and a teacher. Here in the desert, at the Lawrence Ranch, or even in the blue roomed inn, I could allow myself to be the lover, the Native American, the Jew, the Catholic, the wanderer and the writer, the women in D. H. Lawrence's novels.

I would end my journey with a trip to the simple church of Chimayo, which was known for its "holy dirt," providing healing for the ill. My mother suffered in San Francisco from a terrible, mutilating disease. She had worn bright flamboyant colors, big jewelry, and bright red and orange lipsticks. She loved to dress up. I, in contrast, hid my body in muted browns and grays. Now I was alive, once more, in the sultry heat of New Mexico, inspired to write, and to bring her holy dirt, in the hope that she would return to her former self. I wanted my young beautiful mother back. Perhaps the dirt would resurrect her as my spirit was resurrected in, the desert, the Lawrence Ranch, and Taos.

I watched a woman scoop up the dirt gingerly and pour it into a special bag as if it were gold. People came from all over the state and the country to collect this healing dirt; they rubbed themselves with it, they prayed over it, they brought it to those who needed healing. I hoped this holy dirt would help my mother. I asked the woman who noticed me observing her.

"Will this help my mother?"

"If you believe, it will help," she answered.

I brought the dirt to my mother in San Francisco. She smiled when I gave it to her, and I told her the story of Chimayo Chapel. I wanted her to receive some of that sacred space of New Mexico: the red Chile peppers that appeared everywhere, the pinks and golds of the desert, the stark simple crosses on the chapels and churches, the bright blue of the hotel room and the cloudless sky, the white moon in a dark starry night. My mother died a year later. Did it help heal her?

I know my pilgrimage helped me heal as I remembered the eccentricity of Saki, Lawrence's cabin and his erotic paintings, the blue, blue rooms of La Fonda de Taos, and the town of Taos. I prayed at Chimayo Chapel for my mother, for my husband, for my two children, for me to continue to take in D. H. Lawrence's spirit who was similarly changed by the light and feel of New Mexico. I felt confident that I would return there to write and become the writer that I knew I could be.

Sweet Pastry and Coffee: 2006

I have returned home. It is my mother's birthday. It feels right to be in her native country in her hometown in Israel in my favorite bakery café on Ben-Yehudah Street in Tel-Aviv. I am three blocks from the ocean, and the heat of the day has not hit yet. A cool breeze envelops the city before the oppressive humidity makes it impossible to be out for long. The city is alive: buses run, people rush to work, mothers hold their children tightly by the hand taking them to day camps, a large truck with a Coca-Cola sign passes by, and two teenagers dressed in fashionable jeans showing off their stomachs cross the street. In contrast to the city's movement, this café is an oasis. It has been here forever, at least since I lived in Israel and that was over thirty years ago.

My mother and I sit here often eating pasties and drinking strong coffee. The same elderly woman (could it be the same?) is in charge: a heavy-set Russian Polish woman who speaks Russian to her employees. Her daughter seems to be her major worker. The pastries sit on shelves on display: the cheese borekas (knish), spinach, the potato ones with some sesame on the shell, the ones filled with chocolate or meat, and ones filled with poppy seeds. I can't find those pastries in the States; they just don't exist. It is like being in a time machine; nothing has changed. I have lived outside this country, my mother's homeland in chosen exile in San Francisco for the last thirty years. Here in this café, time stands still. French music plays in the background, a woman lights her cigarette as she sips her espresso. I continue to watch the landscape of people and realize it is a very different reality than the one I remember. A female Ethiopian soldier passes. She is striking, with her exotic good looks and sharp army uniform and seems as at home here as any soldier: this is a new face of Israel. The Ethiopian Jews did not live here thirty years ago and have experienced many ups and downs in their immigration here. A religious soldier with a yarmulke on his head waits for a bus. I see more and more religious soldiers and more people who identify as religious. A young father with a baby bottle in his pocket rushes by, pushing his baby in the stroller. Fathers are taking more control of being providers here, too.

The elderly Russian Polish owner barks orders to her daughter who is at the cash register. More people come in to buy coffee and cake. They sit at tables outside or in the café with a newspaper or a cigarette. Some speak on cell phones. It is Israel in a different time; the owner has passed the legacy to her daughter, New waves of immigrants move into the country changing the texture and flavor and forcing the mainstream to take notice of other races and faces, the religious have become more of a majority than a minority, and family roles have changed. It is no longer just the mother taking care of the children. French music plays in the background and the sound of Russian and Hebrew being spoken mixes with the music and the sounds of the traffic. I savor my strong sweet coffee and the variety of small pastries on my blue china plate. I am grateful to be here. Happy Birthday, Mom. I love you.

On a Tour Bus in Jerusalem

Looking out the bus window
ancient stones mix with memories
desert wind on my face
on the back of a motorcycle
in love with this city, this country and a blonde, blue-eyed Israeli
who would not live to see 25.

The sound of church bells
wailing of prayers from mosques
mournful chanting of Jews shrouded in their holy shawls
A younger me:
twenty years ago.

For others on this bus
in Israel for the first time
Jerusalem, a bizarre, exotic city framed
in the guide's historical
monotone.

I want to escape into the deep blue sky of my youth
blend into the cool, gray and white stones
smell the aroma of burnt coffee in early morning
hear the shouts of vendors of Friday afternoons in the "shuk."
I am part of the crowds, their sweat, their pain, their love.

The heat of midday smothers me
as I remember anticipating kisses in the dark,
the mounting excitement of our meeting.

Now he is a statistic in a war begun on the holiest day
during the Yom Kippur War of 1973
of silence and reflection broken by the piercing sound of sirens
freezing our movements, our thoughts, our kisses.

His lungs shatter like glass into tiny pieces.
Yet he remains perfectly still
intact, beautiful, untouched,
no signs of trauma, of blood, of any wound.

Can I forget?
not in this city
not in this country
where memory is part of the cool, gray Jerusalem stone,
the desert heat, the gravestones that adorn the countryside,
the prayers in Hebrew, Arabic, English, Greek or Russian.
No one forgets here.

A Holy Place

It was not just that cloudless blue sky but the quality of the light. It bathed Jerusalem as truly gold. If I were an artist, I would try to paint it and I have seen only glimpses of it in the Bay Area on those hot autumn nights near the ocean at twilight. Of course, in San Francisco the ocean and the beach take on that mystical quality, whereas in Jerusalem it bathes the entire city-- both ancient and modern, the conglomeration of religious sites, Russian Orthodox domes or the Holy mosque of Dome of the Rock where Abraham was said to have sacrificed Isaac and Mohamed appeared, churches of all Christian denominations, and the Western Wall surrounding the Old City. The Wall is the foundation wall of the Second Temple built by King Herod and destroyed by the Romans in seventy AD. It is the one of the most sacred sites in Judaism and is only yards away from the sacred Muslim site the Dome of the Rock, and the places where Christ was born, the Church of the Holy Sepluchure.

I loved Jerusalem from the first moment I first lived there. It is a love affair that has never ceased and continued to ignite. I am as passionate about the city and the golden pink light of its hills with the accompanying scent of jasmine, pine, or eucalyptus, as I was when I first got there. It is a lover I cannot manage to forget. I am reminded of Jerusalem whenever I smell burned coffee. The streets were not yet crowded with the surge of humanity of every type: the religious Jews with their black coats and hats, Arabs dressed in traditional dress and women carrying enormous baskets on their heads on their way to market or onto a bus. Nuns or priests rush to Mass, young soldiers with heavy guns over their arms or strapped on to their backs who are no more than eighteen or nineteen years old wait for buses, or the ordinary Israeli in sandals and shorts and white shirts and sexy women dressed in strapless, flimsy summer dresses and high heels, hurry to do their shopping.

But in early morning when I walked the streets at eighteen years old, the streets still belonged to me and the strong smell of burned coffee pervaded. A year and a half later, I would walk those streets and feel the promise and possibility of being young, in love with a young man, and in love with the city and the country. Later, I would mourn that same young man killed in a war.

Jerusalem is not only holy but frenetic. It includes the intensity of war, the possibility of suicide bombings, and the presence of so many faiths living side by side in a century old city which bombards you in all its sensual delight: the sound of church bells ringing, the sound of the wailing of the Mosques inviting those to pray, the sound and sight of Jews moving back and forth in prayer at the Wall touching it lovingly and placing prayers between its crevices.

I could never tire of it. I looked for solace, respite, and quiet in a city that blared with noise and chaos. I found it one day in a French Catholic church in a part of the city nestled in a valley. The nuns sang the service and as I sat in the back of this lovely church listening to them, I realized once again how holy this place was. I was Jewish in a French Catholic convent listening to sweet voices singing in French. I had found a moment of peace. When I think of Jerusalem, I think of the special light that infuses the city, the smell of burned coffee in early morning, and lastly, that moment in a church where the nuns gave me comfort.

Back in Germany: 2006

I could not believe the heat. How does one land in an international airport in the summer in oppressive humidity with no air conditioning? We waited for a wheelchair to help my husband to the airport hotel in Frankfurt on our way to Israel, and it seemed like they forgot about us. Perspiration dripped down; I felt drenched and he was sweating as well. I worried about the effects of the heat on him since heat exacerbated multiple sclerosis symptoms. In my broken German, I asked one of the attendants how long it would take for a wheelchair to arrive since it seemed like we were waiting for quite awhile. He answered impatiently that there were a lot of other passengers who needed help. I looked around and saw no other disabled passengers but felt it might not be advantageous to argue, so we continued to wait. Finally, a wheelchair arrived, and we began our sweaty journey towards security, the passports check, and then to the hotel. We would rest there for a day before going on to Israel.

I had lived in Germany for six months when I was ten years old. Germany aroused lots of images and memories: castles and forests, winding tree lined streets, amazing pastries, marzipan and chocolate, the endless variety of sausages with names like bratwurst or knackwurst, and the German school where I had been the only Jewish child to ever attend. I also remembered finding silverware in our furnished apartment on Kapellan Strasse with swastikas on the handles, or seeing programs on television about concentration camps. It was the first time I had seen camps and pictures of emaciated, naked inmates or actually learned about the Holocaust. It was ironic for a Jewish child to learn about the Holocaust right from the source: German television. I tried to imagine as a child how this could happen, and how it could happen right where I was living.

My father, who had been born in Germany, and escaped to Palestine at the age of eight, never lost his fascination with his native homeland. He had found a job there that took us to Germany, though we only lasted six months. I learned to speak German then and became an excellent German student in high school, but it had been years since I spoke. It was difficult getting sentences out, although it was exhilarating to realize that remnants of the language lingered and had not left. Words emerged like old friends I had not seen since childhood. |

"Enschulding sie, wo ist die hotel, und wo gehen wir jezt?" I had not forgotten after all as I asked where the hotel was and how to get there. As we made our way, an attendant from Lufthansa pushed my husband, and I followed. I asked him where he was from. He was Iranian and had lived here since he was little with his family. He spoke both Parsi and German perfectly. Did he feel prejudice?

What was it like to be dark skinned and living in Germany? I knew that I had been one of the few dark skinned students in a sea of blonde and lighter skinned German schoolchildren. I remembered asking Vera, one of my new friends at the school, if she had heard of Hitler and whether or not she knew what he done to the Jews. Poor Vera. She had no idea what I was talking about. Our attendant answered that he was attending university here, and he did not feel intolerance.

The airport was modern and impersonal. It could have been anywhere, except for the fact that it didn't have air conditioning. I wanted to exit the airport and experience the streets, speak more German, feel my childhood, and get my parents back for a brief moment in this place where we lived as exiled Jews who tried to return and belong somewhere they no longer belonged. I could not go back. That exile was final.

Across Borders: 2007

A few years ago before school let out, I bid my colleague from Lebanon a warm farewell as she and her family prepared for their summer trip. She taught French at the Catholic school in Menlo Park where I taught English. I joked that since I was leaving for Israel at the same time, perhaps we could meet in Beirut. I had heard Beirut labeled as the Paris of the Middle East, and that it was a charming city by the sea similar in some ways to Tel-Aviv. Wouldn't it be something if meeting in Beirut was not just a fantasy but a reality?

A month into my trip during the summer of 2006, war broke out in Lebanon and Israel became the enemy. The Israeli army was bombing both civilian and military sites, and I worried about my friend's safety. Now, it was not just a matter of humor or wistful thinking about peace in the Middle East, but a real person sat in Beirut with her ten month old son, and she was a friend, a fellow teacher, someone I knew and cared about. I watched television and saw Americans evacuated out of Lebanon to ships and then to Cyprus. I hoped she was among them. It was not until I returned to San Francisco that I heard she was still trapped in Beirut, trying to get out. It took a few more weeks, but eventually, she made it back safely with her son. She was, however, not the same person who left on an ordinary family trip home. She had experienced what it felt like to be a refugee, and to leave with one suitcase and her son at a moment's notice.

I wondered if she would hate me, or remember our discussions prior to the Israeli invasion of Lebanon. I had experienced a nostalgic return to Israel after a ten year absence and felt the incongruity of walking through the chic, fashionable district of Tel-Aviv with its numerous restaurants, boutiques, and sexy men and women with the newspaper headlines about the Israeli soldiers who had been kidnapped precipitating the war with Lebanon.

Israel was always about war and ordinary life colliding. The country bustled with life and shopping and plans and cafes and at the same time families were notified of their son's death or disappearance. Parents worried about their children not making it home because of a potential suicide bomber.

My friend wrote me from Lebanon. War had intruded on her life and in the midst of trying to organize her life around the simple events of going to the beach, family dinners, and meeting old friends, showing off her new son; she needed to worry about her safety and the safety of her son.

A few weeks later, she found herself on a narrow bridge in the cold dark night in a line to get on an American ship. People pushed and shove as an American soldier called out on a microphone trying to calm the crowds; he begged them to stop pushing. He threw bottles of water to people. Fourteen hours later, an amphibious landing shuttle arrived to transport the accepted evacuees to a larger ship outside Lebanese waters, and two hours later, she approached an enormous military ship, the "USS Nashville." Tents were set up and blankets offered. How did it feel to leave your country from the deck of an American military ship?

When my friend returned to Menlo Park, the night on the ship might have seemed like some other life. She was back in the safety of her suburban, American life. Our friendship survived, and it was not about being Lebanese or Israeli. I was just happy that she was back. I had in a symbolic way crossed that bridge, with her. Lebanon was not just a foreign country or newspaper headlines anymore.

I have not stood on a military ship with a child in my arms on a cold dark night, but I have stood at a funeral in Israel for thousands of young men killed in war. We both struggle with our identities. Are we Lebanese? Israeli? American? Christian? Jewish? Muslim? Who are we?

We are never truly separated from Lebanon, from Israel, or from war. We both experience a deep sense of belonging to a part of the world that does not make it easy for us to love it and often force us to leave. When will we be able to visit Lebanon or Israel and not worry about war? When will we be able to meet each other at a café in Beirut or Tel-Aviv? When can we truly be Semitic sisters without borders?

God Moments: 2010 (Israel)

The train whistles
as we pass dilapidated
shacks and red roofs
dry brown earth
small green trees
contrasting the noise and towers
of Tel Aviv.
Yesterday's massage with a woman named Noga
both of us confessing our grief and pain in a small,
sheltered room to the sounds of New Age music as the city throbs.
She speaks of her sister dying after childbirth
and how she, childless and barren, has made it her mission
to help the husband care for the infant.

I tell her about my boyfriend killed during Yom Kippur.
We speak in Hebrew, her hands piercing deep into my body,
in that small, incense scented, room away from war and a young
woman's death and a sister's grief.

I read to her every day, she said.
I am not religious, but I read Psalms to her every day.
It was the only thing I could think of, she whispers.

At the front of the train to Beer Sheva
a young man prays with tefillin as he chants quietly to himself
swaying with the motion of the train.
He is the only one to pray.
Others read, sleep, and look out the window
But I am mesmerized by his ability to pray on a train
without embarrassment, shame or fear.
He is oblivious of everyone, only of his communication
with God.

This is a God moment,
on the way to the desert city of Beer Sheva (Abraham's well)
where our sons study.
Soon, the tall buildings of the university and downtown appear
as if out of nowhere in this dry, barren landscape of desert.

A radio blares,
the man finishes praying
the train whistles
the soldier across from me deep asleep,

and I remember walking down a Tel Aviv street
just yesterday,
and finding a park and a synagogue in the courtyard,
away from the shops and the restaurants and the honking
of cars and cabs and well dressed Israelis,
just me in this park with a closed synagogue
in the middle of the city.

I found myself wading in the sea
looking at the sky
the blue, blue water and blue, blue sky
the café with yellow umbrellas behind me
so grateful for this moment of solitude and grace
my feet caressed by the water.

Thoughts of the man praying on a train
of my fiancé killed during Yom Kippur
of my husband wounded in the same war not far away
of my sons studying at the university that just opened
when I lived in Beer Sheva over thirty years ago
of Noga whose sister died
of colors and memories of stories.
My mother told me about growing up in Tel Aviv,
of my own wounds and my own love for this country,
no matter where, a café, a beach, a train, a park
trying to freeze the moment through
the poem,
the story,
the prayer.

Made in the USA
Middletown, DE
12 December 2022

18073361R00054